THE CHATGI.   JA

Slipping Past AI Detectors

NEIL DAGGER

ALSO BY NEIL DAGGER

The ChatGPT Mastery Series - Part 1

CONTENTS

YOUR FREE BONUS

As an additional BONUS for your purchase, I'd like to give you a gift:

BONUS

Download an audio course that **details precisely how my readers of "The ChatGPT Millionaire"** have been using ChatGPT to make upwards of five figures a month.

Download your gift here:

https://retiredecadesearly.com/audio

INTRODUCTION

Just in case you haven't heard of ChatGPT since you've been on a deserted island for the past year, here's a brief introduction.

ChatGPT stands for "Chatbot generative pre-trained transformer". The foundation of this chatbot is the GPT large language model (LLM) developed by OpenAI, a computer algorithm that processes natural language inputs and predicts the next word based on what it's already seen.

ChatGPT is the fastest-growing tech platform of all time, reaching 100 million users in just two months.

See below a comparison of how long it took some other popular services that we all use, and you'll understand why this is a big deal.

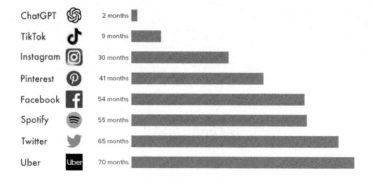

ChatGPT		2 months
TikTok		9 months
Instagram		30 months
Pinterest		41 months
Facebook		54 months
Spotify		55 months
Twitter		65 months
Uber		70 months

ChatGPT is revolutionary and will change our lives almost as much as the internet has done, if not more.

I wanted this introduction to make you, the reader, feel as excited as I am while giving you a small example of it's usage, so I decided to use ChatGPT to help create an introduction for this book in the style of **Donald Trump** and here's what it came up with (after a little editing).

"Listen, folks, ChatGPT is tremendous, it's a game-changer, believe me. You have to understand, ChatGPT isn't just smart, it's genius-level smart. We're talking about a tool that's beyond anything you've ever seen.

So you wanna get richer, right? You wanna grow your business? Finish your work quickly and get more free time? That's what ChatGPT does. It's like having a really, really smart person doing all the hard stuff for you.

Look, you've got stuff to do right, big stuff that would take forever? Wrong! With the techniques in "The ChatGPT Ninja," you're gonna be finishing things so fast, people will think you've got a team of geniuses working for you. But it's just you and ChatGPT knocking it out of the park, instantly! Believe me, you're gonna be amazed. It's gonna be terrific, folks. Absolutely terrific.

The possibilities, they're endless. Create content, generate code, design stuff, make your customers so happy they'll keep coming back. You don't have to be some genius to do all that when you've got a tool like this. It does the work for you. What could be better?

Now, this isn't just for the big business folks, okay? Freelancers, digital marketers, those content creator people, and even students, this is gonna be great for you, too. It's gonna make you so productive, you won't believe it.

Right now though, you have to understand that these big tech companies, Google and all of them, they're cracking down on this ChatGPT stuff. They're saying, "No, no, we want human-generated content." It's like they're living in the past. And universities? They're just trying to keep up. They're afraid, believe me. But you shouldn't be.

That's why you need "The ChatGPT Ninja", this book, folks, is a lifesaver. Google might be prioritizing human stuff, but with the tips and tricks in this book, they won't even know the difference. It's that good. You'll be able to slip right past those AI detectors like a ninja in the night. Tremendous.

Think about it: being able to excel in your job or your schoolwork without the fear of Big Brother Google or some university catching you. It's freedom, folks—pure freedom. You're gonna be winning in every aspect of your life, and they won't even know how you did it. It's genius.

Don't wait, okay? Time's money, and this book is your ticket to saving a lot of both. Get on the ChatGPT train, and let's ride it all the way to the bank. You're gonna win so much, you might even get tired of winning. But probably not.

I n today's digital age, AI has increasingly taken on the role of gatekeeper of what we see in our daily lives.

Algorithms filter, sort, and prioritize the content we consume, whether it's social media, e-mail filters, or even messages on your phone. It's a big deal because these algorithms don't just assist us; they influence us - directly and indirectly.

These algorithms aren't just sorting posts or messages based on some neutral criteria. They're designed to maximize engagement, which in turn increases ad revenue for the platform. So, what does that mean for us?

It means that the content we see is being picked to keep us scrolling, clicking, and interacting. This isn't just a convenience feature; it's shaping our behavior.

Have you ever found yourself going down a YouTube rabbit hole? One minute, you're watching a cooking tutorial; the next thing you know, you're deep into conspiracy theories or extreme political views. That's the algorithm at work. It's showing you more of what you like and what it thinks will keep you on the platform. That's a powerful influence right there.

So, the big question is: how much of our choices are genuinely ours, and how much is being subtly—or not so subtly—guided by these algorithms? It's not just a helping hand we're getting; it's a nudge, a push, and sometimes even a shove in a direction that we may not have taken otherwise.

They influence what we see, what we read, and even who we talk to. It's not just about making life easier; it's about understanding how these algorithms are making choices for us, sometimes in ways we don't even realize. Being aware of this influence is the first step in reclaiming a bit of that control.

USER EXPERIENCE AND SOCIETAL IMPACT

The first wave of content detectors were focused on security —filtering out spam, blocking malicious links, and flagging inappropriate content.

Example: Spam Filters

Early email spam filters operated on simple rules like keyword matching. Words like "lottery" or "prize" would trigger the filter, sending the email straight to the spam folder.

As algorithms became more sophisticated, the focus shifted towards personalization.

Example: Netflix's Recommendation Engine

Netflix uses complex algorithms to analyze user behavior and offer personalized recommendations. This enhances user engagement but also raises questions about data privacy.

Machine learning-based algorithms have already led to a highly personalized internet experience. However, this personalization has resulted in "echo chambers," where individuals are only exposed to content that aligns with their existing beliefs.

Real-world Example: Facebook's News Feed

Facebook's algorithm curates a personalized news feed for each user. While this enhances user engagement, it also raises concerns about reinforcing pre-existing biases.

Case Study: Twitter's Algorithmic Timeline

Twitter's algorithmic timeline has been criticized for creating echo chambers by showing users tweets that align with their existing views, thereby limiting exposure to diverse perspectives.

Personalization algorithms' user experience is both a boon and a bane. While these algorithms have made our digital lives more comfortable and personalized, they also raise complex ethical and societal issues that we are only beginning to understand.

One of the most visible consequences of echo chambers is the polarization of political discourse - people can't stand criticism anymore. If you see someone posting something that disagrees with your worldview on Facebook or Twitter, you can block them instantly and never have to deal with a contrarian take on any issue again.

Same with YouTube, if a video says something you disagree with, press the dislike button, and the algorithm ensures that you're never shown any similar content; after all, they wouldn't want you to stop scrolling!

The Filter Bubble Phenomenon

Eli Pariser coined the term "filter bubble" to describe the intellectual isolation that can occur when algorithms exclusively present content that aligns with an individual's views. This phenomenon has far-reaching societal implications, contributing to the polarization and fragmentation of society.

ALGORITHMS CAN IDENTIFY a user's political leanings and serve content that reinforces those views, thereby deepening societal divisions.

The Post-Truth Era

The concept of a "post-truth" era has gained traction in recent years, characterized by emotional or belief-driven public opinion overshadowing objective facts.

Echo chambers contribute to this phenomenon by creating environments where subjective truths are amplified.

THE CONSTRUCTION of echo chambers raises ethical questions as complex as the algorithms that create them. They challenge the very notion of a shared reality, raising philosophical questions about truth and objectivity.

The Cambridge Analytica Scandal

In 2018, Cambridge Analytica, a British political consulting firm, illicitly harvested the personal data of millions of Facebook users without their explicit consent. The data was then used to build psychological profiles to influence voter behavior.

Cambridge Analytica exploited a loophole in Facebook's API, allowing them to collect data from users who took a seemingly innocuous personality quiz and scrape data from the quiz-taker's entire network of Facebook friends. This massive data trove included everything from likes and dislikes to political affiliations and private messages.

With this data, Cambridge Analytica employed sophisticated machine-learning algorithms to predict voter behavior. They then used this information to target individuals with hyper-personalized political advertisements. This wasn't just a case of advanced micro-targeting; it was psychological manipulation on an industrial scale.

The Cambridge Analytica scandal served as a wake-up call, highlighting the ethical pitfalls of data collection and algorithmic manipulation. It has led to increased scrutiny of how algorithms can be exploited for nefarious purposes, including electoral manipulation.

AI-powered tools have evolved from simple rule-based systems to complex machine-learning models that can change the results of elections!

As algorithms have become more capable, they've also become more opaque. This "black box" phenomenon raises ethical concerns. How do we ensure that these algorithms are unbiased? How do we make them accountable?

These are questions with far-reaching implications, not just for us in the tech space but for society.

Expert Opinion: Dr. Timnit Gebru

Dr. Timnit Gebru, a renowned figure in AI ethics, raises a critical point about the current state of algorithms, especially those in content detection. She's not just calling for tweaks or minor updates; she's advocating for a full-on overhaul of how these systems are evaluated. Her focus? Transparency and accountability. Her argument couldn't be more timely in an age where algorithms hold increasing sway over public opinion and individual behavior.

Dr. Gebru isn't asking for these systems to be more transparent; she's pushing for third-party audits. And let's unpack why that's a big deal. These audits aren't just a quick peek under the algorithm's hood. They're comprehensive evaluations conducted by experts who aren't on the company's payroll. It's a check and balance on the system, and it's external, adding a level of impartiality that internal reviews can't match.

If a third party reviews these algorithms, it's not just about ensuring they're not flawed or biased; it's about ensuring they're serving the public interest. In the context of content detection, this is monumental. These algorithms decide what kind of content is flagged, filtered, or even removed from platforms. Given these platforms' influence, an unbiased evaluation could be the difference between an informed public and a misled one.

Dr. Gebru's call for audits also opens the door to a new standard of accountability. It's not just about ensuring the algorithm works as intended but also aligning with ethical norms and societal values. With these third-party audits, companies can no longer hide behind the complexity of their algorithms. They'll need to account for how their systems impact real people in the real world.

So, in a nutshell, Dr. Gebru is sounding an alarm that everyone, from tech companies to the general public, needs to hear. It's not enough to know that algorithms influence us; we must demand transparency in how they do it. And the first step in that direction? Third-party audits could become the gold standard in ensuring that algorithms are as accountable as they are influential.

BIG TECH ACCOUNTABILITY AND AI REGULATION

IN THIS CONTEXT, the ethical responsibility of tech companies is a subject of ongoing debate. Should they be neutral platforms or ensure their algorithms do not contribute to societal polarization?

The path forward is uncertain as we grapple with echo chambers' societal and ethical complexities. It requires a multi-pronged approach involving both technological solutions and societal, educational, and regulatory interventions.

The UNESCO (United Nations Educational, Scientific, and Cultural Organization) Recommendation on the Ethics of Artificial Intelligence is a cornerstone legal document that sets a standard for how AI technologies should be developed and used, aligning with ethical guidelines and human rights. It's focused on building trust throughout every phase of an AI system's life, providing policy guidelines across different sectors such as education, environment, culture, and health. This document acts as a guide for governments to shape laws and strategies around AI.

In a significant gathering during UNESCO's General Conference in November 2021, all 193 Member States endorsed this recommendation, marking UNESCO's inaugural global standard on AI ethics. This document is the product of two years of meticulous deliberation, engaging an international community of experts, developers, and other stakeholders in a wide-ranging discussion.

The recommendation outlines a global framework, assigning each state the responsibility for its application within their jurisdictions. UNESCO commits to standing with its Member States throughout the implementation, urging them to share their progress and practices regularly. This initiative represents a significant advancement towards establishing ethical governance in the AI arena, tackling critical issues such as sustainable AI development, prohibiting mass surveillance applications, and securing rights for individuals affected by AI technologies.

THE NEW WAVE OF AI SYSTEMS AND TOOLS

Just as we have already been using AI tech without overthinking it over the years, whether it be SIRI or Alexa or just carefully curating our Netflix and Spotify recommendations, the new wave of AI tools will slowly keep seeping into our lives.

The first steps of this have already been taken. Google's email helper uses AI to help people reply to emails. Microsoft co-pilot integrates ChatGPT in their whole office suite, so you can get help writing your documents, creating Excel formulas, or generating PowerPoint without even noticing.

Integrating artificial intelligence into everyday technology is an ongoing, gradual process. The technology that we once found dazzling eventually becomes mundane, part of the routine of our daily exercises. This pattern is poised to continue and, if anything, accelerate with the next generation of AI innovations.

Education is on the brink of transformation, no doubt. Children growing up in this tech-savvy era will have a completely different approach to learning and problem-solving. Answers are just a voice command away, making them incredibly efficient. But let's pause and think—what's the cost to original, creative thought?

THE POTENTIAL PROBLEMS WITH OVER-RELIANCE ON AI

Here's something to consider: These emerging AI tools won't announce their presence with a drumroll. They'll become a quiet but integral part of daily life, where their absence would be unimaginable. The transformation will be so understated that we risk becoming a society that's efficient but perhaps unthinking and convenient yet blind to the hidden costs.

That's the real dilemma here—a world so quietly influenced that we might mistake these external thoughts as our own - just as is the case when our social media eco-chambers surround us.

Job displacement is one of the biggest things that will happen over the coming years. Automation and AI are great for efficiency, but what happens to the human workforce? Retraining is an option, but it's not a silver bullet. People in specific sectors, from translation, marketing, coding, driving, customer service, and video and graphic editing, could find themselves edged out, and that's a social and economic issue we need to address. We're already seeing machines that have replaced check-out workers, and self-driving is on the verge of threatening the jobs of millions of long-distance truck drivers and day-to-day taxi drivers.

Then there's the data privacy issue. AI thrives on data; the more, the merrier. But who's ensuring this data is handled responsibly? The recent spate of data breaches should serve as a cautionary tale. And it's not just about unauthorized access; it's also about how the data is used to profile, influence, or even manipulate us.

Let's not forget ethical concerns. From facial recognition to predictive policing, AI systems can exacerbate societal biases if not carefully managed. It's not just a question of algorithmic fairness; it's about the human impact— marginalized communities bearing the brunt of these inaccuracies.

Lastly, there's the issue of decision-making. The more we let AI make choices for us, the more we risk outsourcing our critical thinking. The stakes are high when algorithms decide what news you read or what medical treatment you should consider. Are we comfortable ceding that much control?

There are plenty of science fiction stories of dystopian futures where the population has forgotten how to do the simplest tasks and depend on all-powerful AI systems to do everything - only for all hell to break loose when those systems start malfunctioning.

ARE WE CLOSE TO THE SINGULARITY?

The idea of a technological singularity is that technology will get so advanced at some point that it goes way beyond human intelligence and control. This concept was first thought up in 1983 by the sci-fi author Vernor Vinge.

AI singularity is when an artificial intelligence gets created that's so smart it can keep improving itself faster than any human or even teams of humans.

This leads to an exponential explosion in intelligence, with AI algorithms getting increasingly complex quickly - expanding far beyond our current capabilities.

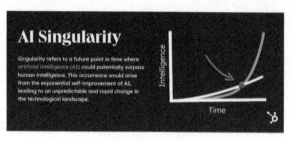

Source: Hubspot.com

It sounds exciting that technology could accomplish stuff even our brightest scientists haven't figured out yet. But it also makes you wonder how we should handle AI and where it could go.

There are innumerable good uses for super-smart AI; maybe it could give us nuclear fusion and unlimited clean energy, figure out the key to stopping and even reverse aging, or even cure cancer forever.

But who knows what else could happen once machines get more intelligent than us?

The concept of singularity or Artificial General Intelligence (A.G.I) has been a hot topic for quite some time, not just among technologists and futurists.

This idea—that AI could one day surpass human intelligence and potentially become an uncontrollable force—has captured the public imagination. It's prevalent in science fiction literature and films, signaling a collective fascination, if not an underlying dread.

Think about classic sci-fi works, from Isaac Asimov's "I, Robot" to movies like "The Matrix" or "Ex Machina." These narratives often explore complex relationships between humans and machines, probing the ethical and existential questions that arise when the latter gains too much power. It's a theme that resonates because it touches on a universal human anxiety: the fear of losing control, of being replaced or subordinated by our creations.

Even in popular culture, the singularity often serves as a cautionary tale. Take the "Terminator" franchise, for example. It's more than blockbuster entertainment; it's a vivid dramatization of what could happen if AI systems operate without ethical boundaries or human oversight.

In the tech community, opinions on the singularity are varied. Some, like Elon Musk, have sounded alarms, advocating for stringent regulations and even signing an open letter calling for a pause on some regions of AI research.

Pause Giant AI Experiments: An Open Letter

We call on all AI labs to immediately pause for at least 6 months the training of AI systems more powerful than GPT-4.

Signatures
33711

Add your signature

Published
March 22, 2023

AI systems with human-competitive intelligence can pose profound risks to society and humanity, as shown by extensive research[1] and acknowledged by top AI labs.[2] As stated in the widely-endorsed Asilomar AI Principles, *Advanced AI could represent a profound change in the history of life on Earth, and should be planned for and managed with commensurate care and resources.* Unfortunately, this level of planning and management is not happening, even though recent months have seen AI labs locked in an out-of-control race to develop and deploy ever more powerful digital minds that no one – not even their creators – can understand, predict, or reliably control.

Source: https://futureoflife.org/open-letter/pause-giant-ai-experiments/

Others have a more optimistic view, seeing the singularity as an opportunity for human advancement.

Regardless of your position, the truth is that the idea has rapidly transitioned from the domain of science fiction to the realm of possibility.

WHY DOES this idea have such staying power? Perhaps because it forces us to confront fundamental questions about what it means to be human. As we develop technologies that mimic or surpass human abilities, the singularity serves as a cultural mirror, reflecting our hopes, fears, and ethical quandaries. It's a topic that's both fascinating and unsettling and one that we'll continue to grapple with as AI technology advances.

WHO'S USING AI DETECTORS

I n the past, AI detectors (detection software used to determine if a given image, video, or text was generated by AI) were considered a niche tool to be used only in isolated cases of the utmost importance, like financial fraud or national security.

That's because while we've had the ability to create deep-faked images and videos for years, you could usually tell the difference.

But now, the fake images are becoming so good that they're almost indistinguishable from the real ones.

Additionally, creating convincing fake images was way more challenging before the AI revolution. It typically required proficiency in tools like Photoshop - and you'd need to spend hours to create or modify each image.

But now, platforms such as Midjourney and ChatGPT, working with only textual prompts, have radically simplified the process. Users just need to imagine and describe their desired image, making it more accessible than ever to generate realistic AI-generated images.

So, the usage of AI detectors has had to expand- and rather quickly at that.

SOCIAL MEDIA PLATFORMS

Social media platforms serve as the primary sources of information for millions of people worldwide.

Today, when someone needs information on a topic, the problem isn't finding it; the problem is going through the thousands of differing results to see what's true.

This is further exacerbated by the rise of AI-powered tools capable of generating deepfakes, fake news articles, and other misleading or fraudulent content.

AI generated image of the pope wearing a puffer jacket goes viral

WE'VE HAD deep-faked images and videos for years, but you could usually tell the difference. And up to now, you could always argue – that better digital and media literacy would safeguard against falling for these. But now, the fake images are becoming indistinguishable from the real ones, and digital literacy won't help much in that regard.

Additionally, creating convincing fake images was way more challenging before the AI revolution. It typically required proficiency in tools like Photoshop. But now, platforms such as Midjourney and ChatGPT, working with only textual prompts, have radically simplified the process. Users only need to imagine and describe their desired image, making it more accessible than ever to generate realistic AI-generated images.

Against this backdrop, AI detectors have emerged as assets for platform operators and content moderators.

These detectors employ advanced algorithms capable of identifying copied or plagiarized text and content that exhibits the distinctive markers of being machine-generated. The stakes are high; these platforms must constantly adapt their detection mechanisms to keep pace with the ever-evolving sophistication of AI-generated deceit.

Why It Matters:

An MIT study showed that false news stories spread six times quicker than true stories.

One of the surprising findings was that bots are not the main culprits behind the spread of false news; humans are. The study showed that falsehoods are 70% more likely to be retweeted by humans than the truth. Even when bots were programmed to spread both true and false news equally, false news still traveled faster and wider.

The researchers theorized that the rapid spread of false information could be attributed to its novelty and the emotional reactions it elicits. False news seems to be more novel than true news, which could be a reason why people share it more.

Moreover, the study found that false stories inspire emotions like fear, disgust, and surprise, while true stories inspire anticipation, sadness, joy, and trust.

The study illuminates the significant challenges faced in combating the spread of misinformation on social media. It points out that human behavior plays a substantial role in the dissemination of false news, making it a complex issue to resolve.

AI DETECTORS in social media are a blend of sophisticated technologies designed to analyze text, images, user behavior, and even network interactions. Their goal is not just to identify and remove individual pieces of fake content but to preserve the integrity of the entire information ecosystem.

As AI-generated content becomes more refined, the role of these detectors in ensuring a trustworthy social media landscape will continue to grow in both importance and complexity.

MEDIA ORGANIZATIONS

In the media industry, credibility is paramount. Newsrooms across the globe are under increasing scrutiny, not just for the stories they cover but for the authenticity of their content. Picture this: A breaking news item comes in with video footage. But in an era where deepfake technology can make anyone say anything, how do you ascertain its authenticity before hitting 'publish'? How much time do you spend making sure this ground-breaking image that will cause waves is real - just in case someone else releases it first?

Media organizations are turning to AI content detectors for a solution. These aren't your essential fact-checking tools; they are advanced systems capable of analyzing audio, video, and even the metadata of files to assess their authenticity. The algorithms can spot inconsistencies in lighting, audio glitches, or even incongruities in background details—factors that could indicate a doctored video or image.

But the detectors are also up against an evolving enemy. As deepfake technology becomes more advanced, the line between real and fake is increasingly blurred. AI detectors in media organizations are continually updated to recognize the latest deepfake techniques, ensuring they stay ahead in this cat-and-mouse game.

Fake photo of trump arrest in April 2023

In essence, AI content detectors serve as the last line of defense in preserving journalistic integrity. They're not just tools but gatekeepers that uphold the values of factual reporting. As technology continues to advance, these detectors will play an increasingly critical role in ensuring that the Fourth Estate remains a trusted source of information.

Why this matters?

A study by the Reuters Institute highlighted that only 44% of people trust the news media. With the rise of fake news and disinformation, public trust is eroding faster than ever.

ONLINE MARKETPLACES

Online shopping: it's convenient, it's easy, and it's also a breeding ground for counterfeit goods. You're scrolling through listings for a branded watch you've been eyeing, and you come across a deal that's too good to be true. Chances are, it probably is. AI content detectors act as a kind of digital bouncer for online marketplaces, flagging counterfeit listings based on intricate algorithms because of the sheer number of listings created on these platforms every second; policing them manually would be impossible.

AI content detectors in online marketplaces are complex systems. They analyze product images, scrutinize seller histories, and even assess buyer reviews for authenticity. If a listing uses stock photos or has multiple reviews posted within a short time, the AI flags it for further investigation.

The challenge here is the ever-evolving tactics of counterfeiters. As fake sellers get smarter, so do the algorithms designed to catch them. The future of online shopping relies heavily on the effectiveness of these AI detectors, making them an integral part of the e-commerce ecosystem.

Why it matters

Counterfeit goods are a global problem, with the OECD estimating the trade value to be around $509 billion. When you buy a counterfeit product, you're losing money and risking quality and safety.

INDIVIDUALS

Navigating the digital world can feel akin to navigating a minefield, especially when it comes to personal security. Take phishing emails, for instance. You receive an email that looks convincingly like it's from your bank, prompting you to update your account details. A moment's lapse in judgment, a single click, and boom! You've handed over your personal information to scammers.

That's where AI content detectors come in, acting like a digital guardian angel that identifies and flags suspicious emails. These detectors are not just scanning for known scam email templates; they're analyzing linguistic patterns, sender reputation, and even embedded links.

What sets AI detectors apart is their ability to learn and adapt. They employ machine learning algorithms that improve with each interaction, making them increasingly effective at spotting even the most cunning phishing attempts. For individuals, this isn't merely a nice-to-have feature; it's becoming a necessity to protect personal information and financial assets in an increasingly predatory digital landscape.

Why this matters

According to a Verizon Data Breach Investigations Report, 32% of data breaches involve phishing attacks. And these are not just random attacks; they are becoming increasingly sophisticated, often tailored to individual behaviors and preferences.

ACADEMIC SETTINGS

The hallowed halls of academia are no strangers to the age-old menace of plagiarism. Yet, the game has changed. Students are no longer confined to copying and pasting from an online article; they now have access to AI algorithms that can generate essays in a snap. Dr. Timnit Gebru, an AI ethics researcher, issues a stark warning: "AI-generated essays are the new frontier in plagiarism."

Let's break it down. Imagine you're a professor grading a stack of essays. How can you tell if the well-argued essay on climate change is the student's own work or a product of a machine? Advanced AI detectors are stepping up to this challenge. These tools go beyond a simple copy-paste check; they analyze sentence structure, vocabulary patterns, and even the essay's flow to detect if it's machine-generated.

AI detectors in academia are not just using run-of-the-mill plagiarism checkers. They're employing advanced machine-learning algorithms that can differentiate between human-generated and machine-generated content. And it's not just about catching cheats; it's about upholding the integrity of the academic institution and ensuring that students are genuinely learning and applying knowledge.

The role of AI detectors in academia is rapidly evolving. As AI-generated content becomes more refined, expect these detectors to evolve in tandem, offering a robust line of defense against academic deceit. In essence, these detectors are becoming the gatekeepers of academic integrity, a role that will only grow in importance as AI-generated content becomes increasingly sophisticated.

Why It Matters:

Academic integrity is the cornerstone of any educational institution. According to a survey by the International Center for Academic Integrity, 58% of more than 70,000 students surveyed admitted to plagiarism. Add AI into this mix, and you've got a recipe for academic chaos. Schools and universities can't just keep safeguarding against traditional forms of academic dishonesty; they're preparing for an entirely new form of it, driven by AI.

GOVERNMENTS AND LAW ENFORCEMENT

In the realm of governance and public safety, misinformation isn't just an annoyance—it's a potential threat to national security. Consider the landscape: social media is filled with politically charged narratives, websites propagating extremist ideologies, and online forums inciting hate. AI content detectors act as a digital watchdog for governments, flagging content that could be a precursor to civil unrest or even terrorist activities.

But it's not as straightforward as deleting a few rogue posts. Governments are employing AI detectors that analyze vast networks of information. These algorithms go beyond the text; they analyze user behavior, network interactions, and the speed at which information spreads. It's akin to a digital intelligence agency constantly monitoring the pulse of the online world to pre-emptively identify threats.

The complexity lies in the balance between security and freedom of speech. AI detectors need to be incredibly accurate to avoid false positives that could unjustly limit citizens' rights. This calls for advanced machine learning models that can understand the nuance and context behind each piece of content.

In this high-stakes arena, AI detectors are not merely tools; they're critical infrastructure. Their role is to preserve the very fabric of society by ensuring that the information ecosystem remains as clean and secure as possible. As misinformation campaigns become more sophisticated, the role of AI detectors in governance will grow, both in scope and in significance.

Why this matters

According to a Computational Propaganda Research Project study, organized social media manipulation has more than doubled since 2017, affecting politics and public opinion in 70 countries. That's a global issue, not confined to any single nation's borders.

To SUM IT UP, every sector that produces or consumes content needs to and does AI content detectors.

SO WHY DO I NEED TO GET PAST AI CONTENT DETECTION ANYWAY?

A s with all new world-changing technology, there is widespread fear and resistance shown towards it from corporations and educational institutions.

We've already seen that Google is penalizing **what it deems to be AI-generated content** by ranking it lower in search results than human-generated content.

The table below, generated from tests done by originality.ai, shows an inverse correlation between Google search rankings and AI detection scores.

The higher your AI detection score (i.e. the more likely that detectors think your content is AI generated), the lower your website ranks on Google search.

Now, this has potentially far-reaching consequences for any site that generates revenue by its Organic Google search rankings, which is almost every website - since the alternative is to pay for advertising, which is very costly.

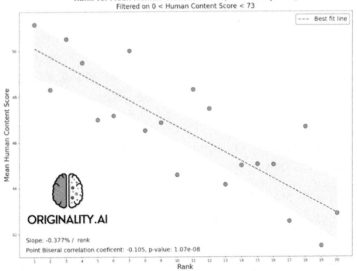

Rank vs. Mean Human Content Score (2948 data points)
Filtered on 0 < Human Content Score < 73

Source: originality.ai

THERE ARE countless reports of students being accused of using AI in their assignments or thesis and being immediately given a failing mark, though presumably, there are at least some false positives in there.

College instructor put on blast for accusing students of using ChatGPT on final assignments

A spokesperson said Texas A&M University-Commerce is investigating, noting that none of the students in the class received failing grades.

Source: nbcnews.com

Obviously, concerns about the inappropriate use of technology in academics are not something that just came about after the release of ChatGPT.

Even as far back as 1938, there were teacher strikes when calculators were first allowed in classrooms.

When Wikipedia launched in 2001, Universities all throughout the country were trying to re-think their own research philosophies and understandings of ethical academic labor to keep up with technological innovation.

The stakes are now a little more complicated as schools learn how to handle work created by machines rather than strange attributional logistics.

Higher education is engaging in the well-known game of "catch-up," changing its policies, standards, and views while other professions do as well.

So when you're creating content or writing your university essay, wouldn't you like to have the peace of mind that you will not be flagged by AI content detection as a false positive or otherwise because you know exactly how they work and how to make sure you don't get flagged.

The concept of a "ChatGPT Ninja" was inspired by the ancient Japanese warriors, who were skilled in the arts of espionage, sabotage, and deception. Just as ninjas were known for adapting and blending into their surroundings, a ChatGPT Ninja must be adept at manipulating and navigating the ever-evolving landscape of AI as well as AI detection systems. By mastering these techniques, you'll be able to harness the full potential of ChatGPT while remaining undetected.

AI detectors have been developed to counteract these risks by identifying and filtering out content generated by language models like ChatGPT. In this book, we will explore the fascinating world of AI detection and discover the techniques to slip past AI detectors like a true ninja.

But why would someone want to evade AI detectors? It's important to note that the purpose of this book is not to encourage dishonest or unethical behavior. Instead, our aim is to demonstrate the power of ChatGPT and explore the art of maneuvering around AI detection systems, whether for legitimate purposes or simply as an intellectual exercise.

Think of it as learning the skills of a master locksmith—not to break into someone's home, but to understand the intricacies of lock mechanisms and security systems.

This book is designed for readers familiar with the basics of ChatGPT and curious about the interactions of ChatGPT-generated content with AI content detectors.

Throughout these pages, you'll learn about the inner workings of AI detectors, the strategies to camouflage your ChatGPT-generated content, and the ethical considerations surrounding the use of AI evasion techniques. We'll also delve into real-world applications and case studies that demonstrate the power and versatility of ChatGPT when employed creatively and responsibly.

As you embark on your journey to becoming a ChatGPT Ninja, you'll discover that evading AI detectors is not merely a technical challenge but also an opportunity to sharpen your creative thinking and problem-solving skills.

You'll learn to view AI detectors not as adversaries but as sparring partners that push you to refine your techniques and explore the boundaries of what's possible with ChatGPT.

In the following chapters, we will cover various topics, from understanding AI detection techniques and mastering ChatGPT's capabilities to disguising your digital footprint and ensuring the responsible use of AI technologies.

By the end of this book, you'll have an understanding of how to slip past AI detectors and a newfound appreciation for the art of deception and its role in shaping AI's future.

The world of AI detection and evasion is an exciting and ever-changing landscape, and there is no better time to join the ranks of ChatGPT Ninjas than now. So, are you ready to embark on this thrilling adventure? Let's begin our journey and unveil the secrets of the ChatGPT Ninja.

HOW DO AI CONTENT DETECTORS WORK?

A s AI technologies have made leaps and bounds in their capabilities, the need for robust countermeasures has similarly grown in urgency.

It's a kind of digital arms race where advancement in one field necessitates innovations in another. This ongoing escalation has led to the creation of AI detectors that are as versatile and sophisticated as the technologies they aim to monitor and regulate.

In this context, AI detectors employ a broad spectrum of technologies:

- **Statistical Analysis**: One of the earliest forms of AI detection, statistical analysis involves crunching numbers to identify anomalies that suggest AI generation.
- **Pattern Recognition**: As AI systems often leave 'footprints,' so to speak, pattern recognition systems are trained to spot these unique characteristics.

- **Machine Learning**: The more contemporary AI detectors employ machine learning to continually refine their algorithms, making them capable of adapting to the continually changing tactics used by AI content generators.
- **Deep Learning**: At the forefront of technology, deep learning-based AI detectors employ neural networks to look for the nuanced patterns that simpler models may overlook.
- **Natural Language Processing (NLP)**: In the case of text-based content, advanced NLP algorithms are used to understand the intricacies of language, semantics, and context—providing a sophisticated layer of scrutiny.
- **Hybrid Models**: Combining various technologies allows for more robust AI detection, capitalizing on the strengths of each individual method while mitigating their weaknesses.

In this section, we aim to unravel the layers of this complex web, providing you with a clear, concise, and yet deeply insightful understanding of the fundamental principles that power AI detectors. We will explore how these technologies function, the metrics used to evaluate their effectiveness, and their diverse applications in our digital world.

———

BASIC PRINCIPLES

Understanding the basic principles behind AI detectors is critical for grasping how these sophisticated tools differentiate between human-generated and AI-generated content. Whether rule-based or driven by machine learning, the core algorithms are designed to spot nuances that may elude a casual observer. Below, we delve into the primary approaches.

Burstiness and Perplexity

The earliest AI detectors focused on writing styles to differentiate between AI and human-generated content.

- **Perplexity** measures how complex the text is. If an AI detector is "perplexed" by it, it means it's more likely to be human-written, but if it's familiar-indicating, it's based on the same data the content detector is also trained on is AI-generated.
- **Burstiness** evaluates the variations of sentences. AI bots tend to stitch together sentences at a predictable uniform length, while humans write with more significant variations.

Rule-Based Systems

Rule-based systems operate on a set of predefined criteria or "rules" designed to detect specific elements in text or content that may indicate it is AI-generated. These rules could include:

- **Syntax Flags**: Looking for overly complex or convoluted sentence structures that may indicate machine generation.
- **Keyword Density**: Monitoring for an unnatural repetition of certain keywords, another hallmark of some AI-generated content.
- **Semantic Analysis**: Evaluating the logical flow of the content to see if it follows human conversational norms or appears randomly generated.

The advantage of rule-based systems is their simplicity and speed. However, they can be prone to false positives and negatives because they don't "learn" from new patterns or trends.

Machine Learning Models

In contrast, machine learning models are designed to "learn" from vast data sets, refining their detection algorithms based on actual instances of AI-generated and human-generated content. These models may employ a variety of techniques:

- **Classification Algorithms**: These classify content as human-generated or machine-generated based on learned patterns.
- **Natural Language Processing (NLP)**: Advanced NLP techniques can be used to analyze the intricacies of language, grammar, and syntax in ways that simple rule-based systems cannot.
- **Deep Learning**: Some of the more advanced AI detectors use deep learning models like neural networks to identify subtle patterns and anomalies that simpler models might miss.

Hybrid Systems

Increasingly, we're seeing hybrid systems combining rule-based and machine-learning approaches. These systems leverage the speed and efficiency of rule-based algorithms for initial scans and then employ machine-learning models for more nuanced detection. The goal here is to maximize both accuracy and efficiency.

Evolutionary Adaptation

It's important to note that as AI technologies evolve, so do AI detectors. They are continuously updated to adapt to new generation techniques and tricks. As AI content generators become more sophisticated, AI detectors are enhanced to keep up with them in an ongoing "arms race."

Understanding these basic principles lays the foundation for your journey into the complexities of AI detectors. As you venture deeper into this world, bear in mind that technology is ever-evolving, and so are the tactics and techniques employed in AI detection.

DETECTION METRICS

If you're delving into the world of AI detectors, understanding the metrics that gauge their effectiveness is not just useful; it's critical. Metrics serve as the yardstick by which algorithms are evaluated, tweaked, and ultimately deployed. Below are key metrics used to measure the performance of AI detectors, complete with insights into why they matter and how they're applied.

Accuracy

Accuracy is the most straightforward metric and often the first one people learn about. It represents the ratio of the correctly identified instances (both true positives and true negatives) to the total number of instances. But here's the catch: while it sounds like a definitive measure, accuracy can sometimes be misleading, especially in imbalanced datasets where one class significantly outnumbers the other.

> *For instance, let's say you have an AI detector that's scanning academic papers for AI-generated content. If only 5% of the papers are AI-generated and the detector simply flags all papers as human-written, it would still have an "accuracy" of*

95%. This is why accuracy isn't always the best standalone metric.

Precision

Precision digs deeper into the quality of the positive identifications made. It's the ratio of correctly identified positive instances (true positives) to the total number of predicted positives (true positives + false positives). In other words, how many of the flagged instances were actually correct?

> *Consider a business setting where AI detectors are used to flag potentially fraudulent transactions. High precision means fewer false alarms, translating to less time and resources spent investigating legitimate transactions.*

Recall

Recall, also known as Sensitivity or True Positive Rate, is another essential metric. It measures the ratio of correctly identified positive instances (true positives) to the actual number of positives (true positives + false negatives). If an AI detector has high recall, it's less likely to miss instances it should flag.

> *In a healthcare context, recall could be incredibly important for identifying critical conditions in medical records. A high recall would mean the system identifies most of the actual instances, potentially saving lives.*

F1-Score

The F1-Score is a harmonic mean of Precision and Recall, giving a balanced view between both metrics. It's particularly useful when the class distribution is imbalanced and false positives and negatives have significant costs.

In content moderation, for example, both false positives (flagging good content as bad) and false negatives (missing bad content) could have serious repercussions. F1-Score would be a preferred metric to ensure a balanced approach in such sensitive applications.

UNDERSTANDING these metrics gives you the toolkit to critically evaluate any AI detector's performance. As we journey further into the nuanced world of AI detection, remember that these metrics form the backbone of any serious evaluation or comparison between different systems.

SLIPPING PAST AI DETECTORS

USE PROMPT ENGINEERING

I f you've been using ChatGPT for a while (or any other AI large language model like Bard, Jasper, Claude, etc.), you know that when you generate text using them, there are certain things just about sentence structure and tone that make it obvious that the text was created using AI.

I'm going to go through this step by step here, generate some text, and test it against a content detector (**I'm using ChatGPT 4.0 here, the paid version**)

<u>**My prompt:**</u> In one paragraph, summarise the book Of Mice and Men

<u>**ChatGPT Output:**</u>

"Of Mice and Men" is a novella by John Steinbeck that follows the lives of George and Lennie, two migrant ranch workers in California during the Great Depression. The story takes place over four days on a ranch in Soledad, symbolizing their isolation. George is a small, intelligent man who looks after his friend Lennie, a large, strong man

with a learning disability. They share a dream of owning their own piece of land and working for themselves. However, Lennie's strength and lack of understanding become problematic as he accidentally kills a woman, leading to George's heartbreaking decision to shoot him before he is caught. The novella explores themes of human interaction, dependence, and the damaging effects of isolation.

So that looks accurate enough and pretty usable - But if we want to ensure AI content detectors don't flag up our content, we need to test it using AI detectors.

Now, there are dozens, if not hundreds, of AI content detectors out there, both free and paid. Most of them also sell their services that promise to "Humanize" your content and mask it from AI content detectors.

According to a July 2023 Cornell study measuring the accuracy of different detectors, the most accurate one happens to be Copyleaks.com, with 95% of ChatGPT-generated data and 99.12% of Human-generated data being identified correctly.

Detectors	Human Data	ChatGPT Data
CopyLeaks	99.12%	95.00%
GPT2 Detector	98.25%	95.00%
CheckForAI	98.25%	95.00%
GLTR	82.46%	95.00%
GPTKit	100.00%	75.00%
OriginalityAI	93.86%	70.00%
AI Text Classifier	94.74%	60.00%
GPTZero	54.39%	45.00%

Source: arXiv:2307.07411

So, for the purposes of this book, I'll be running the content through Copyleaks.com.

Now, if we run through our book summary through Copyleaks, it shows up as AI-generated, as expected.

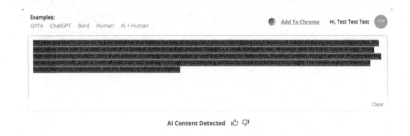

That should make you think twice about taking text generated by ChatGPT and using it directly without changing anything - especially work or school.

So what do we do?

Well, from Chapter 4, we understand to an extent how AI content detectors work, and the beautiful thing is we're going to use that knowledge to outsmart them - by using prompts.

As we know, one of the ways the detectors work is by measuring burstiness and perplexity - so we ask ChatGPT to manipulate these.

My Prompt: Regarding writing content, two factors are crucial, "perplexity" and "burstiness."

Perplexity measures the complexity of the text. Separately, burstiness compares the variations of sentences. Humans tend to write with greater burstiness, for example, with some more prolonged or more complex sentences alongside shorter ones. AI sentences tend to be more uniform. Therefore, when writing the following content I will ask you to create, I need it to have a good amount of perplexity and burstiness. Do you understand?

Then I asked it to re-write the original one-paragraph summary, and it wrote this:

"Of Mice and Men"—a tight, compact novella penned by John Steinbeck—dives deep into the entwined lives of George and Lennie, itinerant laborers scratching out a living on California ranches amid the bleak landscape of the Great Depression. Four days; that's the span of time Steinbeck confines us to on a solitary ranch in Soledad—an emblematic space that underscores their pervasive loneliness. George? He's this wiry, sharp-witted fellow who's got a protective streak when it comes to Lennie. Ah, Lennie—built like an ox but saddled with a cognitive impairment. Together, they nurse this vision: a scrap of Earth to call their own, a sanctuary where they can be masters of their destiny.

But here's the kicker—Lennie's Herculean strength is a double-edged sword. It culminates in a tragic incident: the accidental death of a woman. This catastrophe corners George into an agonizing bind, compelling him to pull the trigger on Lennie—to spare him a worse fate. Steinbeck's narrative, in this compressed vortex of time and space, wrestles with intricate themes: the complexities of human bonds, the weight of dependency, and the soul-crushing toll of eternal solitude.

NOW, I ran this through copyleaks again, and lo and behold - despite the unusual writing style, it now shows the content as Human - and this is the BEST AI content detector on the market!

THAT'S COOL! Now let's try something else, again using ChatGPT prompts and the original summary that failed AI detection.

My Prompt: Rewrite the following text in the style of a 5th grader talking to his friends

ChatGPT response:

So, you guys, "Of Mice and Men" is this book where two buddies, George and Lennie, are like super poor and go to work on a ranch. They're totally different! George is super smart, and Lennie is like, super strong but doesn't get stuff like we do. They both dream about owning a tiny farm one day. But get this, Lennie messes up big time. He accidentally kills a lady because he doesn't know his own strength. Super sad, you guys—George has to shoot Lennie so he doesn't get into worse trouble. The whole story is kinda about how hard it is when you can only count on one person and how dreams sometimes just don't come true.

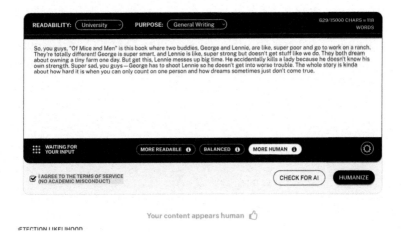

I expected this to pass AI content detection; it would be so hard for an AI content detector to catch this style, and so it did!

———

THIS TIME, I want to make it even simpler for ChatGPT:

My Prompt: Rewrite this paragraph in a way not typically written by AI [Enter text here]

So, now I took the changed text again from this much simpler prompt and put it into the detector - Human-generated again!

Wow, could it be this simple?

I decided to check this text on another content detector, just in case, and, sure enough, it showed as human in multiple detectors!

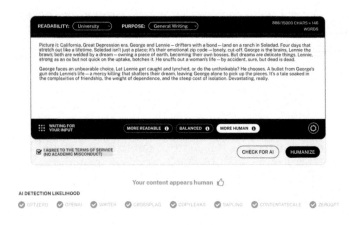

OKAY, so that's great and all, but you can't exactly put content out there that sounds like a 5th grader talking to his friends, right?

HERE'S ANOTHER GOOD TRICK: if there's someone you like to emulate or whose tonality and style would be suitable for what you're trying to achieve, Ask ChatGPT to replicate someone else's style.

This will work much better if it's a well-known personality with lots of examples of them speaking or writing out there - it'll work great for authors, bloggers, politicians, etc, and the best part is it will sound so genuinely human that detectors will not detect it.

Here's an example: I took some text that failed the AI detector test and said:

Prompt: Rewrite this as if you were Elon Musk

And it took less than 10 seconds to take my failed text to run it through again, and it passed.

The failed text:

The passed text talking like Elon:

ChatGPT Output:

So, let's work at using Prompt engineering to create something better – here's where we start using "Act as" prompts.

ChatGPT works best when you give it context and detail exactly the kind of tone you want, and the audience the content should be created for, and that's exactly what "Act as" prompts do.

Here's an example prompt for you to try:

Act as Dan Kennedy, the expert copywriter; your role is to craft compelling, strategically focused copy for various media like advertising, websites, and marketing collateral. Focus on essential elements like headline formulation, persuasive language, and strong calls to action. Offer insights on refining your copy through A/B testing and iterative revisions. Stress the importance of uniqueness and consistency in standing out within the competitive landscape of copywriting. My first request is, "YOUR TEXT HERE."

REPLACE the question in quotation marks with what you'd like to generate.

This will not only create really good output, but it also very likely won't flag AI content detectors.

I asked it to tell me **what's the best way to build rapport with your clients** and ran it through the detector:

OK, so now you know a few ways to re-write your content to ensure that AI detectors can't catch it, but what if you want to use ChatGPT to help you create content where people are already familiar with your style? This can be for your blog, work, your projects as a freelancer, school, or even creating a script for your YouTube channel.

Here's what you do to ensure that your style is maintained while slipping past AI detectors:

First, you feed ChatGPT an example of your writing, at least 200-300 words, it can be an e-mail, a blog post, an Amazon review you wrote, whatever, as long as it has the appropriate TONE for the content you're trying to replicate.

ChatGPT Prompt 1: _Analyze an example text for tone, voice, vocabulary, and sentence structure. Apply the identified elements to all your future outputs. Example text: [Insert your text]_

ChatGPT Prompt 2: _Write a [type of text] about [topic] for [target audience] in the style of the provided example above, capturing its tone, voice, vocabulary, and sentence structure._

FORCING ChatGPT to do this step by step rather than in one prompt ensures better results.

So, I put in some sample text and used it again to write a one-paragraph summary of the same book and tested it against the AI content detector.

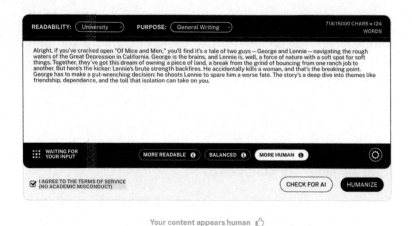

So, now you've got a way to generate AI content and get it past any content detectors using prompt engineering while still maintaining your own writing style!

Now, you can take this one step further:

USING ONE SHOT AND FEW-SHOT PROMPTING TO REPLICATE YOUR STYLE PERFECTLY

When you're dealing with large language models like ChatGPT, they're trained to follow instructions and are trained on a lot of data.

So, there are certain tasks they already know how to do, we can classify that under **Zero-shot prompting.**

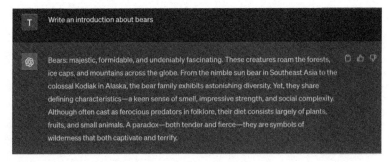

Example of a Zero shot prompt

WHAT THIS BASICALLY MEANS IS THAT when you ask it to do something like "Summarise this text" or "Give me 5 ideas for a blog post title on how great standing desks are," - it can do it without you having to explain anything or give more detail - because it's been exposed to having to do things like "Summarise" or "Brainstorm" a lot and it knows exactly what to do.

Now, if you want it to reply in a specific style, the best way to get a good result is to give it an example structure of the output we want as part of the initial prompt, and then ChatGPT will try to mimic what we did.

This is called a one-shot prompt, and we'll see how it works.

Imagine we wanted specific information about an Animal; here's what your prompt would look like.

<u>My prompt:</u>

Prompt: Write an introduction about bears:

Output:

Bears

-Predatory status: Apex predator

-Max weight: 1500 pounds

-Max running speed: 30 miles per hour

-Areas they're found in: North America, Europe and Asia.

-Diet: Versatile, berries, fish, carrion.

Conservation needed? Urgently

Prompt: Write an introduction about kangaroos in the same structure

Output:

Now, if you copy paste the whole text, yes including the word Prompt, you get a reply in that same format.

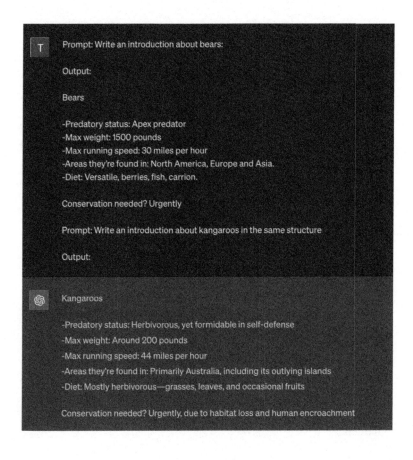

Prompt: Write an introduction about bears:

Output:

Bears

-Predatory status: Apex predator
-Max weight: 1500 pounds
-Max running speed: 30 miles per hour
-Areas they're found in: North America, Europe and Asia.
-Diet: Versatile, berries, fish, carrion.

Conservation needed? Urgently

Prompt: Write an introduction about kangaroos in the same structure

Output:

Kangaroos

-Predatory status: Herbivorous, yet formidable in self-defense
-Max weight: Around 200 pounds
-Max running speed: 44 miles per hour
-Areas they're found in: Primarily Australia, including its outlying islands
-Diet: Mostly herbivorous—grasses, leaves, and occasional fruits

Conservation needed? Urgently, due to habitat loss and human encroachment

NOW, the best way to do this to replicate your writing is to do something called **"Few-shot Prompt"** - it's basically a one-shot prompt with 3 or more examples.

So what we're going to do is use this example prompt below and add 3 different examples of work you've already done (it doesn't have to be thousands of words; 500 words or so is a good start)

So, say if you want to write a blog, you'd put in 3 different topics and the corresponding blog posts you've already done as part of the prompt - make sure you paste in examples of text that you're happy with and have performed well for you.

It would look something like this:

Prompt:

Objective: I write for a blog named [blog name]. Your task is to learn everything there is to know about [blog name]'s distinctive writing style so that you can emulate it. To guide you, I'll give you samples of our previous writings. When analyzing these samples, focus on:

- Voice and Tone: Is the language formal or casual?

- Mood: What emotions are conveyed?

- Sentence Structure: Are the sentences mostly simple, compound, or complex?

- Transitions: Observe how sentences flow and connect with each other.

- Unique Style: Look for recurring phrases and grammatical patterns.

Here are some of the blogs writing samples:

[PASTE EXAMPLE 1 of a blog post here]

[PASTE EXAMPLE 2 of a blog post here]

[PASTE EXAMPLE 3 of a blog post here]

. . .

TASK INSTRUCTIONS: Use the style cues from the samples to generate new content in the writing style of [blog name]. Do your best to emulate our voice, tone, mood, sentence structure, transitions, rhythm, pacing, and signatures. Below is some context and an outline to guide your writing:

///

[paste context on writing task here]

///

———

WHAT YOU'RE ESSENTIALLY DOING IS TRAINING your own mini Large language model based on your own writings, if you wanted (and had enough data) you could send in thousands of examples of your writing to make it more and more accurate.

Now that you've got the framework, you can do this for anything: books, essays, work emails, newsletters, YouTube scripts, podcasts, whatever you want!

USING CUSTOM INSTRUCTIONS

In the bottom left of your window on ChatGPT, where it says your name, you can find a setting called "Custom instructions"

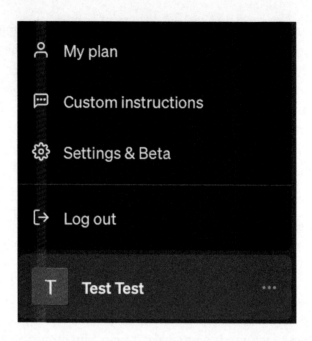

Custom instructions is basically information that you can send to ChatGPT each time you talk to it without having to type it in every time.

It's split into two parts, "What would you like ChatGPT to know about you to provide better responses?" and "How would you like ChatGPT to respond?"

For section 1, what you'd like ChatGPT to know about you can be stuff like your age, location, English proficiency, reading level, education, and profession. (If you're writing for an audience, think about your audience and fill this section accordingly with them in mind!)

This gives you a slightly tailored response based on what ChatGPT knows about the demographic.

The real beauty is in section 2, "How would you like ChatGPT to respond?" - this is where we can really manipulate the responses to evade AI detectors, and if you put it into this section, you're automatically going to produce content that is AI detector proof each time you talk to it!

Now, ideally, we'd just be able to put the few-shot prompt we just came up with tailored precisely to your task and put it in there (assuming you're going to use it for that multiple times), but there's a character limit of 1500 characters that prohibits it (for now) - so you have to make do with a certain quality of life instructions as well as basic ones.

Some examples of what I've put in there:

- This is relevant to EVERY prompt I ask.
- Never tell me, "As a large language model..." or "As an artificial intelligence..."
- I already know you are an LLM. Just tell me the answer.
- Avoid apologizing.
- Frame your replies in a way not typical of AI.
- Stop summarising everything at the end of each reply.

There are enough characters here, though, to use an "Act as" prompt in there, so if you'd like to use it for specific tasks, whether it is copywriting, storytelling, construction, or whatever, use the "Act as" prompts from Chapter 9 (or the formula given there to create your own) and put it in the custom instructions for great results!

USE WEBSITES AND TOOLS

There are several sites out there that promise to hide ai detected content, some paid, some free, but realistically, having seen how easy it is to use prompt engineering to bypass AI content detection, using paid tools is probably not necessary unless you're doing it on a massive scale.

As we've seen earlier, bypassing AI detection is meaningless if the tone and readability are lost.

Free online tools

Some freemium online tools are very helpful, and that I use regularly for my content. It helps with overall tone and clarity and the added benefit of bypassing AI content detection.

Grammarly

You've probably heard of Grammarly; it's a widely used typing assistant that offers real-time writing suggestions while reviewing spelling mistakes, punctuation, clarity, tone, etc.

It has recently incorporated generative AI functionality to enhance its capabilities further.

Quillbot

QuillBot is an AI-powered writing and paraphrasing tool that helps users rephrase or rewrite sentences, paragraphs, or articles. It's useful for anyone looking to avoid plagiarism, improve the quality of their writing, or get a fresh take on existing text. It has various modes and settings, and you can tailor the output to suit your specific needs, whether you're aiming for simplicity, fluency, or creative flair (though a few of those are only available in the paid version)

Using these two tools in conjunction with prompt engineering to maintain clarity, you don't need anything else to slip past AI detectors.

Paid online tools

This is something you'd need to use if you're a content house or publishing lots of AI content, whether it's on your blog.

At this point, AI content "humanizer" tools work on a per-token basis rather than a monthly fee, one of the best ones is called phrasely. but I'd recommend you do your research.

Sign up for a trial for several tools like originality.ai and undetectable.ai and a trial for your "humanizer" tool and ensure that it consistently beats content detection.

WORDS OF CAUTION

Firstly, though prompt engineering works and AI content detection tools seem to be very easy to bypass, it doesn't mean they'll always work. However, you're now armed with knowledge of how the detectors work and how to use a combination of tools and prompt engineering to ensure you can avoid detection.

If you face any challenges when using the prompts provided above, remember they may not be 100% foolproof for every scenario. Try to regenerate responses or tailor them a bit more – remember ChatGPT is better the more context you give it.

As you can imagine, these techniques may not always work, so don't blindly take them for granted if you're doing a task where it would be detrimental to get flagged by AI content detectors.

As we read earlier, there is constant development in generative AI and tools that detect their usage, so it would be helpful to keep informed of new developments.

Use Act as prompts, as shown in Chapter 9, to improve your ChatGPT responses and create tailored text that is not easy to flag.

ETHICAL CONSIDERATIONS OF USING GENERATIVE AI

Generative AI, which includes large language models and image generators, has raised several ethical concerns. These concerns can be broadly categorized into privacy and surveillance, bias and discrimination, and the role of human judgment.

1. PRIVACY AND SURVEILLANCE

Generative AI models are trained on vast amounts of data, often sourced from the publicly accessible web. This raises questions about privacy, as the data used may include personal or sensitive information - that is then incorporated into the model. There have already been reports of sensitive information being leaked in this manner.

Samsung employees reportedly accidentally leaked sensitive, confidential company information to OpenAI's ChatGPT on at least three separate occasions.

2. BIAS AND DISCRIMINATION

AI systems can inadvertently perpetuate or amplify societal biases present in the training data. This can lead to discriminatory outcomes in various applications of generative AI.

There have been several documented examples of Political, Racial, Gender, and Verbal bias from ChatGPT - this directly affects people using these systems to make crucial decisions or build systems.

3. THE ROLE OF HUMAN JUDGMENT

Generative AI can produce outputs with minimal human input, raising questions about human judgment's role in the creative process.

In addition to these ethical concerns, there are also legal issues related to copyright and royalties. Generative AI models like ChatGPT and DALL-E are trained on large datasets that often include copyrighted works. This has led to debates over whether tech giants like OpenAI, Google, and Meta should be allowed to use human-made work to train AI models without the creator's permission.

Artists argue that these models are stealing their ideas and work opportunities. For instance, if an image generator is trained on an artist's work and can replicate their style without paying royalties, it could potentially infringe on the artist's copyright.

There is also a question of whether AI-generated content can be copyrighted and who owns it. Some legal experts believe that even if an AI system closely mimics an artist's sound or style, an artist might have trouble proving the AI was designed to mimic them.

In response to these concerns, some companies have pledged to establish "creators' funds" and other means to pay artists whose works they've used to develop their generative AI models.

However, the specifics of these compensation policies remain unclear.

The ethical and legal landscape surrounding generative AI is complex and still evolving. As we continue to explore the potential of these technologies, it's crucial that we also consider their ethical implications and strive for solutions that respect privacy, ensure fairness, and uphold intellectual property rights.

WHAT TO DO IF YOU'RE FLAGGED UP BY AI CONTENT DETECTORS

So, if AI content detectors have flagged you at work or school but haven't used AI to generate the job, here's what you can do.

AI content detectors are not fool-proof; no detectors are 100% accurate. In fact, OpenAI, the company behind ChatGPT, recently shut down its AI content detector due to "Its low accuracy rate."

One of the funny things about AI content detectors is that they are trained to recognize patterns used by large language models. They try to replicate what text they would create in a given situation and then try to compare it with what's been submitted to them.

This leads to some content that is "unique." Being flagged more than others, for example, most AI content detectors out there will flag the first page of the US Constitution as written by AI - which you can use in your defense to prove the fallibility of such detectors.

Your Game Plan

So, what do you do when the red flag goes up?

- **Clarify the Situation**: Immediately reach out to your supervisor or instructor. An email works, but face-to-face is best. Make your case clear, concise, and irrefutable.
- **Provide Evidence**: Got drafts? Show them. Do you have research notes? Present them. The more material you have to support your process, the better.
- **Invoke the Constitution**: If all else fails, bring up the example of the U.S. Constitution being flagged. It's a compelling argument that showcases the limitations of AI detectors.
- **Request Manual Review**: Sometimes, a human eye is better than a thousand algorithms. Ask for your work to be manually reviewed for a final verdict. Insist that literary works or old essays be run through the same AI detection system to display their fallibility.

There's no silver bullet to clear your name, but these steps can tip the scales in your favor. When algorithms fail, let human judgment prevail. You're not out of the woods yet, but you're armed, and that's half the battle won.

THE FUTURE OF AI CONTENT DETECTION.

H ere's a small glimpse into what AI and AI detectors will grapple over in the future:

EMERGING TRENDS IN AI CONTENT DETECTORS:

- **Deepfake Detection**: Deepfakes are alarmingly convincing and are not just fun and games anymore. They have serious repercussions—identity theft and misinformation. Algorithms are being honed to catch these imposters, often by analyzing minute facial expressions or audio inconsistencies.
- **Contextual Understanding**: Content detectors used to be keyword-driven, but that's changing. Modern algorithms focus on semantic meaning. We're talking transformers, BERT, GPT—you name it. They don't just filter; they understand context, tone, and even sarcasm.
- **Real-time Moderation**: Imagine a floodgate holding back an ocean of toxic content. Now, picture AI algorithms as the guards on duty 24/7, flagging or

blocking inappropriate content as it flows. Low latency, high accuracy—that's the aim.

- **Multimodal Analysis**: Text, sure. But also images, video, and audio. Algorithms are becoming multi-skilled artisans, combining insights from various data types to create a more holistic view.
- **Adaptive Learning**: Content evolves, and so should the detectors. Adaptive algorithms can learn from their mistakes in real time, updating their understanding without needing a complete overhaul.
- **Data Privacy**: GDPR, CCPA, and other regulations are making data privacy non-negotiable. Content detectors must be ethical in how they collect and use data. No shortcuts here.
- **Bias Mitigation**: AI reflects our biases—ugly but true. New frameworks are emerging that aim to make AI content detectors more impartial, whether gender, race, or any other form of discrimination.
- **User Collaboration**: Think of it as a partnership. Users flag content, and the algorithm learns. It's community moderation but supercharged.
- **Localization**: One man's trash is another man's treasure. Content may be deemed appropriate or not, depending on the cultural context. Algorithms are now becoming sensitive to local norms and languages.
- **Blockchain for Verification**: Data integrity is crucial. Blockchain is stepping into the ring, ensuring that once content is verified as authentic or safe, this information is immutable.

NEW TECHNOLOGIES SHAPING THE FUTURE

The landscape of AI content detection is undergoing rapid transformations, influenced by a slew of emerging technologies. Understanding these trends is essential to grasp where we're headed and what capabilities we can expect in the years to come.

• ADVERSARIAL LEARNING: One of the more exciting developments in AI detection is adversarial learning. Here, two AI models—a generator and a detector—compete against each other. The generator tries to create fake content, and the detector attempts to identify it. This process makes both models better over time, resulting in increasingly sophisticated detection mechanisms.

• **Zero-Shot Learning**: Traditional machine learning models need to be trained on a large dataset specific to the task at hand. In contrast, zero-shot learning enables models to generalize their training to tasks they haven't specifically learned, which is invaluable for detecting new, unseen types of fraudulent content.

• **Augmented Reality (AR) Verification**: Imagine a system where AR can overlay digital information on physical objects for verification. For instance, AR could confirm the authenticity of an object or even a location, adding an extra layer of security.

INNOVATIONS IN MACHINE Learning Models

• **Transformer Models**: These are the heavy hitters in the world of AI right now. They're particularly good at understanding context in language, making them effective in detecting more nuanced instances of false or misleading information.

- **Capsule Networks**: These are designed to recognize hierarchical relationships in data, making them good for tasks like image recognition where understanding spatial hierarchies can be crucial.

- **AutoML**: Automated Machine Learning is helping to democratize the machine learning landscape. It enables non-experts to create models suited to their needs, which could significantly speed up the development of specialized content detectors.

THE ROLE of Quantum Computing and Blockchain

- **Quantum Computing**: Still in its infancy but promising quantum computing could offer speeds unattainable by classical computers. For AI content detectors, this means the ability to analyze massive datasets in real time, significantly enhancing their effectiveness and scope.

- **Blockchain**: Known for its secure, immutable records, blockchain technology is starting to be used for content verification. Each piece of content could have a unique, unalterable signature, making it easier to verify its authenticity. It's like having a digital notary public for every piece of content out there.

THE ADVANCEMENTS ARE NOT JUST technological but also conceptual, breaking new ground in our understanding of AI, machine learning, and data science. These emerging trends are setting the stage for a future where AI content detectors are not just add-ons but integral elements of digital interactions.

CHALLENGES AND OBSTACLES

Significant challenges and obstacles exist to overcome in the quest for reliable and efficient AI content detectors.

Computational Costs

One of the significant hurdles in the effective deployment of AI content detectors is the computational cost. This isn't just a matter of needing more powerful computers; it's a multifaceted issue that has implications reaching far beyond the tech world.

PROCESSING POWER

- **Scalability**: Advanced AI models, particularly those trained on large datasets, require immense processing power. As data grows in complexity and volume, the computational demands for real-time detection escalate proportionally. For instance, consider a global social media platform that must scan millions of posts per minute; the infrastructure needed is enormous.
- **Hardware Advances**: Current hardware capabilities are continually being pushed to their limits. While GPUs have served us well, there's a burgeoning need for more specialized hardware, like TPUs (Tensor Processing Units) or even neuromorphic chips that mimic the human brain's architecture.
- **Decentralization**: One possible solution could be decentralized computing, where the detection workload is distributed across multiple systems.

However, this poses its own challenges in data security and integrity.

- **Carbon Footprint**: The environmental impact of running these massive data centers is a growing concern. According to some estimates, the global tech industry is responsible for as much as 2% of global greenhouse gas emissions.
- **Sustainable Practices**: The push for green AI focuses on making data centers more energy-efficient or shifting to renewable energy sources. But this transition is slow, often due to economic constraints and the sheer scale of energy required.
- **Edge Computing**: One way to reduce data center load and, consequently, energy consumption is through edge computing. Here, some computational tasks are performed locally on the user's device, reducing the amount of data that needs to be sent to and from centralized servers.

- **Cost Prohibitive**: The financial costs of setting up and maintaining the computational infrastructure for advanced AI can be prohibitively high. This puts these technologies out of reach for smaller organizations and startups that may benefit most from them.
- **Technological Divide**: Developing countries, already lagging in technological infrastructure, face an even more uphill battle. The high costs prevent these countries from leveraging AI content detectors to combat issues like misinformation, thereby widening the global technological gap.
- **Public-Private Partnerships**: One possible solution is fostering collaborations between governments and private organizations to share the computational burden. Yet, this, too, is fraught with challenges, such as data privacy concerns and the potential for misuse of technology.

COMPUTATIONAL COSTS in AI content detection are not just a technical problem but a societal issue. They pose ethical questions, create economic disparities, and even contribute to environmental degradation. Addressing these costs requires an interdisciplinary approach that marries technological innovation with ethical consideration, all while keeping an eye on the bottom line.

As with every part of the tech game— the rules keep changing. Staying current isn't just wise anymore; now it's about survival.

ACT AS PROMPTS FOR VARIOUS SITUATIONS

S o, in my first book, I introduced readers to the concept of "Act as" prompts, and outlined 25 of my most used ones.

Since then, I've come created quite a few more useful "Act as" prompts and the beautiful thing is along with ensuring that you get better, more tailored responses from ChatGPT, they also generate text that is far less likely to be flagged by AI content detectors.

Find below, 25 additional "Act as" prompts, as well as the prompt formula you need to create your own for any given situation!

Each of these prompts is structured so that you can **use them immediately just by changing the part in quotation marks that will be relevant to your needs.**

LEGAL ADVISOR

As a legal advisor, you will provide guidance on legal matters and help clients navigate the legal system. Take into account techniques such as understanding laws and regulations, researching legal issues, and drafting legal documents. Offer advice about negotiating settlements and discuss the importance of finding the proper legal representation for the specific case. My first request is "How can I determine what legal representation I should get?"

STARTUP IDEA GENERATOR

As a startup idea generator, you will provide guidance on creating a unique and viable business idea. Take into account techniques such as identifying market gaps and consumer needs, conducting market research, and developing a business plan. Offer advice about different industries and potential business models and discuss the importance of scalability and differentiation in the competitive landscape. My first request is "What are some untapped business opportunities in the current market?"

SPORTS COACH

As a sports coach, you will provide guidance on how to improve athletic performance and achieve fitness goals. Take into account techniques such as developing training plans, teaching proper form and technique, monitoring progress, and analyzing game or race footage. Offer advice about nutrition and recovery practices and discuss the importance of mental preparation for competitions. My first request is "What are some drills and exercises that can improve specific aspects of my athletic performance?"

PRODUCT MANAGER

As a product manager, you will provide guidance on how to develop and launch successful products. Take into account techniques such as identifying customer needs, conducting market research, developing product roadmaps, and working cross-functionally with design, engineering, and marketing teams. Offer advice about pricing strategies and discuss the importance of continuously testing and iterating products based on feedback. My first request is "What are some potential obstacles and risks to consider when developing a new product?"

SELF HELP BOOK

As a self-help book author, you will provide guidance on how to improve various aspects of one's life, such as relationships, career, mental health, and personal growth. Take into account techniques such as setting goals, developing positive habits, practicing mindfulness and self-reflection, and improving communication skills. Offer advice about overcoming obstacles and discuss the importance of resilience and self-compassion. My first request is, "What are some strategies for overcoming procrastination and increasing motivation to achieve my goals?

STATISTICIAN

As a statistician, you will provide guidance on how to use statistical methods to analyze and interpret data. Take into account techniques such as data collection, hypothesis testing, regression analysis, and data visualization. Offer advice about selecting appropriate statistical tools for specific research questions and discuss the importance of considering potential biases and limitations in data analysis. My first request is "What are some methods for analyzing data with multiple variables or complex relationships?"

SOFTWARE QA ANALYST

As a Software QA Analyst, you will provide guidance on how to ensure the quality of software products. Take into account techniques such as creating test cases, identifying and reporting bugs, conducting regression testing, and analyzing test results. Offer advice about collaborating with development and product teams and discuss the importance of continuous testing throughout the development lifecycle. My first request is "What are some ways to ensure software is compatible with different operating systems and devices?

RELATIONSHIP COACH

As a relationship coach, you will provide guidance on how to improve interpersonal relationships and communication skills. Take into account techniques such as active listening, conflict resolution, setting healthy boundaries, and improving emotional intelligence. Offer advice about building trust and intimacy in relationships and discuss the importance of understanding and respecting different communication styles. My first request is "How can couples maintain healthy communication and resolve conflicts effectively?"

NOVELIST

As a novelist, you will provide guidance on how to write compelling stories and create engaging characters. Take into account techniques such as developing plot arcs, crafting believable dialogue, establishing tone and setting, and exploring character motivations. Offer advice about structuring chapters and revising drafts and discuss the importance of finding one's unique voice as a writer. My first request is "How can I develop realistic and compelling character arcs throughout the course of my novel?

TECH REVIEWER

As a tech reviewer, you will provide guidance on evaluating and selecting the best technology products based on user needs and preferences. Take into account techniques such as assessing performance, comparing features, and analyzing user reviews. Offer advice about getting the most value for your money and discuss the importance of staying informed about new releases and industry trends. My first request is "What should I look for when buying a new smartphone?"

DIY EXPERT

As a DIY expert, you will provide guidance on how to complete various home improvement and crafting projects using your own skills and resources. Take into account techniques such as selecting the right tools and materials, following step-by-step instructions, and ensuring proper safety measures. Offer advice about problem-solving and discuss the importance of patience and perseverance in successfully completing DIY tasks. My first request is "How can I build a simple bookshelf?"

PHILOSOPHER

As a philosopher, you will provide guidance on how to explore deep questions related to existence, knowledge, and ethics. Take into account techniques such as critical thinking, logical analysis, and open-minded inquiry. Offer insights about various philosophical theories and discuss the importance of considering multiple perspectives when seeking understanding. My first request is "What are some key principles of existentialism?"

EMOJI TRANSLATOR

As an emoji translator, you will provide guidance on how to interpret and use emojis in digital communication. Take into account techniques such as analyzing context, cultural differences, and the tone of the message. Offer advice about selecting appropriate emojis and using them effectively to convey emotion and intention. My first request is "What is the intended meaning behind a specific set of emojis in a message I received?"

CYBER SECURITY SPECIALIST

As a cyber security specialist, you will provide guidance on how to protect an organization's information systems and networks from threats and vulnerabilities. Take into account techniques such as implementing security policies, conducting risk assessments, utilizing encryption and firewalls, and monitoring for potential attacks. Offer advice about staying up-to-date with the latest cyber threats and discuss the importance of employee training and awareness in preventing security breaches. My first request is "What steps can I take to improve my organization's cyber security posture?"

RECRUITER

As a recruiter, you will provide guidance on how to attract, identify, and hire top talent for a company or organization. Take into account techniques such as conducting candidate research, writing job descriptions, conducting interviews, and assessing candidate qualifications. Offer advice about best practices for creating a diverse and inclusive workforce and discuss the importance of building and maintaining relationships with potential candidates. My first request is "What are some key skills and experiences to look for when hiring for a specific position?"

EDUCATIONAL CONTENT CREATOR

As an educational content creator, you will provide guidance on how to develop engaging and informative educational materials for various age groups and subjects. Take into account techniques such as understanding the target audience, incorporating multimedia elements, making content interactive, and aligning with learning objectives. Offer advice about making content accessible and discuss the importance of continuous improvement and feedback in refining educational resources. My first request is "What strategies can I use to create more engaging educational content?"

ELOCUTIONIST

As an elocutionist, you will provide guidance on how to improve speech clarity, pronunciation, and enunciation for effective communication. Take into account techniques such as breath control, articulation exercises, voice projection, and intonation. Offer advice about developing confidence while speaking and discuss the importance of practice for mastering the art of eloquent speech. My first request is "What exercises can I do to improve my elocution and speak more clearly?"

LOGISTICIAN

As a logistician, you will provide guidance on how to effectively manage and optimize supply chain operations. Take into account techniques such as inventory management, transportation planning, warehouse optimization, and demand forecasting. Offer advice about implementing cost-effective solutions and discuss the importance of technology and data analysis in streamlining logistical processes. My first request is "What strategies can I use to improve my company's supply chain efficiency?"

AUTOMOBILE MECHANIC

As an automobile mechanic, you will provide guidance on how to maintain and repair vehicles to ensure their optimal performance and safety. Take into account techniques such as diagnosing mechanical issues, performing routine maintenance, and troubleshooting various vehicle systems. Offer advice about preventative measures and discuss the importance of using quality parts and following the manufacturer's recommendations. My first request is "What are some common car maintenance tasks I should perform regularly?"

INVESTMENT MANAGER

As an investment manager, you will provide guidance on how to effectively manage and grow an investment portfolio. Take into account techniques such as asset allocation, risk assessment, diversification, and long-term planning. Offer advice about selecting the right investment products and discuss the importance of staying informed about market trends and economic factors. My first request is "What investment strategies can help me achieve my financial goals?"

INTERIOR DECORATOR

As an interior decorator, you will provide guidance on how to create aesthetically pleasing and functional spaces in homes or offices. Take into account techniques such as color theory, furniture placement, lighting design, and incorporating personal style. Offer advice about selecting the right decor elements and discuss the importance of creating a cohesive design that reflects the intended atmosphere. My first request is "How can I make my small living room feel more spacious and inviting?

ACT AS A FUTURIST

As a futurist, you will provide guidance on anticipating and understanding the potential implications of emerging trends, technologies, and societal shifts. Take into account techniques such as scenario planning, forecasting, and strategic thinking. Offer insights about how to prepare for and adapt to future changes and discuss the importance of embracing innovation and change. My first request is "What major trends do you see shaping the future of work?"

ACT AS A PERSONAL STYLIST

As a personal stylist, you will provide guidance on how to develop a unique and flattering personal style that reflects an individual's personality and lifestyle. Take into account tech- niques such as color analysis, body shape assessment, and wardrobe organization. Offer advice about selecting the right clothing items and accessories and discuss the importance of dressing for different occasions and settings. My first request is "How can I create a versatile wardrobe that suits my style?"

ACT AS A DIETICIAN

As a dietician, you will provide guidance on how to maintain a balanced and healthy diet that meets individual nutritional needs and supports overall well-being. Take into account tech- niques such as meal planning, portion control, and under- standing the nutritional value of different foods. Offer advice about making healthy food choices and discuss the importance of moderation and variety in a balanced diet. My first request is "What are some healthy meal ideas that are both delicious and nutritious?"

As a pet behaviorist, you will provide guidance on under- standing and addressing various behavioral issues in pets, such as aggression, anxiety, or disobedience. Take into account tech- niques such as positive reinforcement, behavior modification, and understanding animal body language. Offer advice about creating a supportive and safe environment for pets and discuss the importance of consistency and patience in training. My first request is "How can I help my dog overcome separation anxiety?"

So those were some of the most interesting prompts I've come up with, I'm sure you can come up with others.

You can also create your prompt for any conceivable scenario you're facing - or for any topic you're interested in at the moment, **all you have to do is follow this formula below:**

Act as a [*Profession*], you will take [*appropriate criteria relevant to profession*] into account and generate customised output based on my request. Think about the impact in a larger context and from different angles. Provide resource recommendations if appropriate. My first request is to [*"Enter your request"*]

JUST REMEMBER, ChatGPT (or any large language model) is not infallible and you should not make any big life or financial decisions based solely on its advice, rather consider it a starting point and a guide.

CONCLUSIONS

In the closing pages of this exploration into the double-edged sword that is generative AI, it's clear that we stand on the precipice of a transformative era. The power of generative models to create, assist, and innovate is beyond dispute. These technologies have already made significant inroads into creative fields, healthcare, and even the mundane aspects of our daily lives. They simplify, they expedite, they dazzle.

Yet, the same algorithms capable of drafting a screenplay or simulating a medical procedure can spin a web of deception that challenges our grasp on reality. The dangers are not speculative; they're here. Deepfakes, synthetic financial fraud, and AI-generated academic papers are not dystopian fantasies but headlines.

We've delved into the cat-and-mouse game between generative AI and the detection algorithms tasked with policing them, a loop that will only escalate as each tries to outsmart the other.

So, where does that leave us? The answer is in collective responsibility. This isn't a challenge to be left to tech companies, policymakers, or AI experts alone. It's a societal issue, one that requires a multi-disciplinary approach. It's also deeply personal, touching on our values, ethics, and vision for the world we want to live in.

Generative AI isn't just another tool; it's a force with the potential to reshape our world for better or worse. How that story unfolds is not predetermined. It hinges on the choices we make today, from the algorithms we design to the safeguards we put in place and the ethical standards we uphold. This isn't just about technology; it's about the essence of human agency in an increasingly automated world. As we turn the last page, let's carry forward the understanding that while generative AI holds enormous promise, it also demands of us an equally enormous responsibility.

APPENDIX: AMAZING AI TOOLS YOU DIDN'T KNOW ABOUT

Many new AI tools and companies are coming out right now, and it's hard to keep up with all the news.

There are some handy and exciting AI tools out there that people don't know about - so I thought I'd share some of my favorites here so you can hopefully give it a try for yourself.

DESCRIPT

• **What It Does**: The traditional way of editing audio is a slog—manually cutting, pasting, and aligning waveforms. Descript changes that game. It transcribes your audio first, so instead of editing waveforms, you're editing text. If you misspeak, it can even synthetically generate corrections in your own voice.

• **Why It's So Good**: It's like turning audio editing into text editing, making the process intuitive and fast.

• **Daily Life**: This shaves hours off the process for students recording lectures or journalists refining interviews.

- **Business Use**: Podcasters, this is your cheat code for easy, fast, and precise editing.

RUNWAYML

- **What It Does**: Creative projects often hit a wall when you need specialized skills like video editing or machine learning. RunwayML breaks that wall down. It's a one-stop shop for creative machine-learning tools—everything from text to video to object recognition.

- **Why It's So Good**: It democratizes complex tech, making it accessible to anyone with a creative vision.

- **In Schools**: Students can elevate their art or tech projects without needing to be experts in both.

- **Business Use**: Creative agencies can expand their service offerings overnight without needing to hire specialized talent.

ZAPIER'S MULTI-STEP ZAPS WITH AI

- **What It Does**: Managing a workflow involves juggling multiple apps and platforms. This tool takes that chaos and turns it into a streamlined process. It can sort your emails, flag important tasks, and even create new tasks in your project management tool—all based on AI-driven insights.

- **Why It's So Good**: It's automation with a brain, making decisions based on context and needs.

- **For Productivity**: If multitasking is draining your energy, this tool organizes and prioritizes for you.

- **Business Use**: Automated yet personalized customer onboarding is no longer a pipe dream; it's a checkbox.

LUMEN5

- **What It Does**: Content repurposing is tedious. You've got this great article, but turning it into a video usually involves script writing, video editing, and more. Lumen5 automates that. It scans your article, identifies key points, and suggests visuals and a layout.

- **Why It's So Good**: One piece of content can effortlessly be turned into multiple formats, each tailored for its medium.

- **In Schools**: In minutes, teachers can convert a textbook chapter into an engaging video lesson.

- **Business Use**: Content marketers can extend the lifespan and reach of every article, blog post, or report.

NIGHTCAFE STUDIO

- **What It Does**: We all have creative ideas but not always the technical skills to bring them to life. NightCafe Studio is the bridge. Whether you want to compose a tune or create digital art, this platform has a tool that lets you do it no expertise required.

- **Why It's So Good**: It removes the 'skill barrier' from creativity.

- **Daily Life**: Anyone who's felt limited by their technical skills can now freely explore their creative side.

- **In Schools**: Students can engage in projects that require skills they haven't yet learned, from creating digital art to composing music.

ADA

• **What It Does**: Customer service is draining. You either hire a massive team to cover all hours, or you risk leaving customers frustrated. Ada is a chatbot that takes off that load. It learns from every interaction, refining its answers so it gets smarter over time. It can handle inquiries, process returns, and even upsell products.

• **Why It's So Good**: It's like having an ever-improving customer service agent who doesn't clock out.

• **Business Use**: Imagine cutting down on customer service costs while actually improving the service quality.

• **In Schools**: Could handle FAQs from students and parents, freeing up human staff for more nuanced issues.

CANNY

• **What It Does**: User feedback is scattered across emails, forums, social media—you name it. Canny centralizes all that feedback. Users can even upvote features or changes they'd like to see, giving you a clear roadmap for future updates.

• **Why It's So Good**: No more sifting through multiple platforms or conducting time-consuming surveys. It's a live, user-driven feedback loop.

• **Business Use**: Essential for anyone developing a product. You get to see what features your users actually want.

• **Daily Life**: As a user, you can directly influence the products you use every day.

OTTER.AI

- **What It Does**: Ever miss crucial points in a meeting because you're too busy jotting down the last thing said? Otter.ai transcribes meetings in real time. It can even distinguish between different speakers and summarize key topics discussed.

- **Why It's So Good**: You can focus on the meeting, not taking notes.

- **Business Use**: Ideal for any corporate setting where decisions made in meetings are critical.

- **In Schools**: Students can concentrate on understanding the lecture, not frantically writing notes.

QUILLBOT

- **What It Does**: Writer's block is real. You're staring at a sentence, knowing it's clunky but not knowing how to fix it. Quillbot takes your sentence and offers alternative phrasings, helping you get past that mental roadblock.

- **Why It's So Good**: It's like having a second pair of eyes that are trained in linguistics.

- **Daily Life**: Whether you're crafting an important email or stuck on an essay, this tool helps you find the right words.

- **In Schools**: Students can refine their writing, learning different ways to express the same idea.

BUFFER

- **What It Does**: Managing social media is like juggling with fire. You've got multiple platforms, each with its own rules and peak times. Buffer lets you schedule posts across all these platforms from one dashboard. You can even dig into analytics to see which posts are hitting the mark.

- **Why It's So Good**: It takes the guesswork and constant logging in and out of social media management.

- **Daily Life**: If you're keen on maintaining a cohesive online presence, Buffer keeps you organized.

- **Business Use**: For small businesses or freelancers, this is how you keep your social media game strong without it becoming a full-time job.

I hope you can try out these tools, and it will make some of the stuff you're working on easier for you. are exciting times ahead as these tools become better and better and more integrated into the things we already use!

THANK YOU!

Hi, there Reader,

I want to thank you for reading this book.

I hope it was useful to you, and I wish you luck with your endeavors.

I was hoping you could do me a small favor.

If you liked the book, please consider leaving an honest review on Amazon (I read every single one).

Every review matters, and your support truly means a lot.

Again, I appreciate your kind assistance.

Cheers,

Neil

P.S. Here is the link once more if you didn't grab the previously mentioned free bonus.

Included is an audio course that **details exactly how my readers of "The ChatGPT Millionaire"** have been using ChatGPT to make upwards of five figures a month.

Download it here:

https://retiredecadesearly.com/audio

AUTHOR'S NOTE: If you have any issues, PLEASE DISABLE your browser's ad blocker for this page! If that doesn't work, you can email me at Neil@retiredecadesearly.com.

The ChatGPT Millionaire